DEJI DOKUN-FAMUBODE
NEITHER SILVER NOR GOLD
7 SIMPLE STEPS TO A WEALTHY LIFE

First published by Strahlung Innovation & Enterprise Group (SIEG) 2024

Copyright © 2024 by Deji Dokun-Famubode

All rights reserved. No part of this publication may be reproduced, stored or transmitted in any form or by any means, electronic, mechanical, photocopying, recording, scanning, or otherwise without written permission from the publisher. It is illegal to copy this book, post it to a website, or distribute it by any other means without permission.

Designations used by companies to distinguish their products are often claimed as trademarks. All brand names and product names used in this book and on its cover are trade names, service marks, trademarks and registered trademarks of their respective owners. The publishers and the book are not associated with any product or vendor mentioned in this book. None of the companies referenced within the book have endorsed the book.

First edition

This book was professionally typeset on Reedsy.
Find out more at reedsy.com

Contents

APPRECIATION   v
FOREWORD   vi

I   GETTING THE RIGHT PERSPECTIVE:

1   FIRST THINGS FIRST   3
2   UNDERSTANDING WHAT WEALTH IS   6
3   THE PURPOSE OF WEALTH   10
4   THE RIGHT APPROACH TO WEALTH-BUILDING   12

II   SEVEN SIMPLE STEPS TO BUILDING WEALTH

5   STEP 1: DEFINE YOUR VISION OF WEALTH   19
6   STEP 2 - GET COMFORTABLE WITH NUMBERS (BUDGETING)   23
7   STEP 3-CREATE A WEALTH-BUILDING LIFESTYLE (SAVING)   27
8   STEP 4- INVEST (MONEY SHOULD NEVER SLEEP)   30
9   STEP 5 - LEAVE NO WEAPON UNDRAWN (USE ALL AVAILABLE...   33
10   STEP 6 - STAYING WEALTHY (HOW TO ENJOY AND KEEP IT)   37
11   STEP 7 - LEGACY: BUILDING GENERATIONAL WEALTH   40

| 12 | CONCLUSION: A FINAL WORD | 43 |
| 13 | Suggested Reading | 45 |

About the Author   47

APPRECIATION

To Lola,
   thanks for standing by me through thick and thin,
   and pushing me to be the best that I can be

To Honey and Hadiza,
   thanks for the joy you both bring

And to Luqman, my childhood friend
   thanks for reviewing this text,
   and for being a sounding board for many ideas over the decades.

FOREWORD

What is this book about?

I have never really liked the genre of self-help books. Why? Because I don't believe anyone can really know another person's circumstances. We are all unique individuals and accordingly we have unique circumstances. In this sense, a part of me therefore also thinks that the writers of self-help books are mostly on an ego-trip, thinking they know better, trying to fix our lives even when they are not speaking from our own unique experience. Yet, paradoxically, I am writing what could be seen essentially as a self-help manual. Perhaps the "self-help" is the key here? First of all, this is not really a manual, but rather a friendly reminder of simple, natural principles of life which we mostly all already know of but which we often fail to practise and convert into useful habits. I have experienced a transformation in my life by applying these principles, hence why I am confident enough to share them, in the hope that you will have the courage to put in the effort to imbibe these principles and create the helpful habits that will transform your life in the way you wish. If I succeed in inspiring you to do this, I will have made a contribution to life on earth, and would thereby have added to my own wealth too. This book is a reminder that you and only you can help yourself and turn your life into what you want it to be.

Good luck!

I

GETTING THE RIGHT PERSPECTIVE:

UNDERSTANDING THE BASICS OF WEALTH

1

FIRST THINGS FIRST

What Demographic is this book targeted at?

This book grew out of a short presentation prepared for a high school alumni group reunion. I was encouraged by my enthralled colleagues to share it with the world. The average age of that audience was 50 years. However, the principles in this book are applicable to all ages, to anyone who is capable of learning and still willing to learn. I would even encourage teaching these simple principles to children from as early as 5 years old, so they can imbibe and build good habits as well as develop a positive appreciation of money, prudence and delayed gratification from an early age.

(Expected Outcomes) What can you as a reader gain from it?

At the end of this book, you:

- will have greater clarity about wealth; what it is, what it is to be used for and why it is important to build it.
- will have the tools you need to commence your own wealth-building journey and live a fuller, more-assured and more peaceful life.
- will no longer be confused or deceived by the various schemes and

scams out there offering outlandish wealth and wealth-building ideas, based on unrealistic premises and timelines.

How to use this book

I recommend that this short book be read at least twice.

1. First reading – just go through it like a novel, follow the discourse and in your mind, see how the principles apply to your life in general. At this stage, do not study it like a manual, but read it like a conversation between friends, like a chat over coffee, just us. Let your imagination work and don't put yourself under any pressure. This first reading can be done in a day or a week, but probably no longer than a month; you don't want to lose momentum. The language is deliberately non-technical. You don't need a business degree to understand anything in this book. Read it at your own pace, but with a sense of purpose.
2. Second reading – this time read the book as a call-to-action, make notes on the steps you are going to take in order to develop your plan to apply what you have surmised from your first reading and transform it into action, such as the budgeting, saving and planning, etc. Simple action steps are suggested at key points to help you along. After this second more detailed reading, you really won't need to read the book again, except where you need a reminder of certain principles every now and then. A re-cap of the major principles and steps is further offered in the concluding chapter to serve as a quick reference when in doubt. My hope is that by the time you have applied the straightforward principles laid out in this book and implemented the suggested steps for 6 months, you will have imbibed them as lifelong habits and could potentially write a book about the subject yourself. In short, live the dream,

don't read the dream. Taking action is a most important key in a life well lived.

2

UNDERSTANDING WHAT WEALTH IS

I often come across questions about wealth and money. It seems to be a very popular topic and is on the minds of many people. There is also a craze about entrepreneurship these days. Everyone wants to be an entrepreneur. In most cases, however, this desire is not fuelled by an urge to create value for society but is only a wish to become rich, make money. Afterall in classical economics, we are told that the reward for entrepreneurship is profit. That is however not the purpose of it, just a by-product.

Money is not wealth. Although this should already be obvious to the deep-thinking person, it needs to be emphasized that money is not wealth!

Wealth I would define as *"your personal reservoir of material wherewithal"*, the capability to make your wishes and desires come to life on earth.

In many societies in the not-so-distant medieval past, this wherewithal lay in military strength, and the monied merchant class was subservient to the warrior class because their money did not necessarily translate into wherewithal. Going farther back into primeval history, at some point the major wherewithal was the physical prowess which was required to dominate others in the tribe (or indeed neighbouring tribes), to protect kith and kin from wild animals, developed hunting skills etc. This makes it clearer why human beings have always built wealth and why they still need to do so today. It remains an important, even vital task.

However, before we can truly understand the components of wealth, a couple of questions need to be answered first,

1. **Who am I?** i.e. who is the person looking to build wealth? Simple as it may sound, if this is not clear, true clarity on wealth cannot be found. Have you ever stopped to really understand who you are? Regardless of your profession, marital status or race, you are first and foremost a human being. A human being is not the physical body it inhabits. You must have sensed this by now. When you look through your eyes, does it not feel exactly the way it used to when you were 5 years old, even though your body has gone through tremendous changes? Does it not even feel the same when you dream? The real you is obviously an essence within, a consciousness inside the body so to speak. Recognising this is important because it leads to the next question.
2. **Why am I on earth?** If I am not a physical being, what then am I doing on earth? We are on earth to gather experiences, to learn and to grow. We are to learn about and become familiar with natural principles through our efforts to make life on earth better for ourselves and for our fellow men. For example, we come to recognize the Law of Gravity – what is heavy weighs down, what

is light soars. These principles are universal, applicable not just to physics but also to our inner life. So we have expressions like being "weighed down" by problems, as opposed to "feeling light" inside, or looking for a "pick-me-up". This our purpose is why at some point we have to leave the earth (i.e. death) and return to where we came from (let us say a place of higher consciousness?), there to consolidate our learning, wiser and stronger. These are not religious but natural principles, to be found in all civilizations and cultures, they are universal.

With these two main questions answered somewhat, we can already surmise that the primary component of wealth is already given to us as a gift - our physical body, which includes the most advanced tool of all, the brain. This body is our tool for exploring life on earth. The state of your body therefore is the primary measure of your wealth, as well as its foundation. However, the body in itself is useless without that inner essence or energy that powers it (let us call it the soul). The body therefore must remain subservient to your true consciousness which, as your conscience, is also the bastion of your morality and therefore your true energy; otherwise in neglecting your inner life, you will build negative energy which not only leads to a faster deterioration of the body itself but also negates the entire purpose of life alluded to above.

We are also aware that death occurs when the soul departs the body. Even for those who doubt the existence of an inner consciousness, the numerous documented out-of-body or near-death experiences of various people all over the world should give us food for thought.

Now while I do not want to dwell on the topic of the soul, I am conscious that it is also a topic that interests many people, especially those who might have become dissatisfied (like I was) with the various explanations offered to us by religion. At the end of this book, I will share details of a book I have read, which in my opinion offers crystal-clear, non-religious clarity on life and existence. It is well-worth reading if you are interested.

3

THE PURPOSE OF WEALTH

In the preceding section, we defined wealth as the "reservoir of material wherewithal" and we have somewhat identified our purpose for being on earth. Wealth, we can thus infer, is to facilitate life on earth, a capability to make the earth a better school, a place of love and peace, both in particular (i.e. for yourself) and in general (i.e. for your fellow human beings). We need this wherewithal to do the following:

1. **Provide Shelter** - This is more than a house or apartment (including all the facilities that make your life comfortable), but also includes those things that make it possible for you as an individual to unfold your innate abilities. For example, if you are an artist or sound engineer, you perhaps need a studio to work in. This is part of your home, your base, the place where you prepare for your engagement with the world.
2. **Provide Nourishment**- this includes not just food and drink, but all things you need to nourish and sustain your body and maintain your physical and mental health (medicines, herbs, exercise equipment, treatments, etc)

3. **Provide Clothing** – this goes beyond keeping you warm or covering your nakedness, but includes clothing as an expression of your true nature. You need the wherewithal to dress as suits your personality, to cloak your body according to your own sense of beauty and aspiration.
4. **Acquire Experience** – You need wherewithal to facilitate the full experiencing of life on earth, e.g. to travel, to interact with others, to buy books, art and other things that help you explore this beautiful life.
5. **Build a Legacy** - wealth gives you the ability to leave a mark on the earth and make it a better place even after your departure, this does not have to be a foundation or scholarship endowment or a museum. It could be as simple as wealth giving you the ability to sustain yourself and still have ample time to mentor others, to pass on wisdom to your grandchildren, to help nourish talent in your community, to serve your society, to write poetry, to teach, etc. Remember that the purpose of life on earth is to make it a better place and in so doing grow inwardly and find happiness.

4

THE RIGHT APPROACH TO WEALTH-BUILDING

There are some natural principles of life that a builder of wealth must understand and imbibe in his life, in his daily life. Modern society, especially in the Western world, tries to upend these natural principles to the benefit of the few who have a measure of control over the masses. It is important to recognize the distortions and strive towards correction in your own life.

I will highlight the aspects of this approach but please note that though intertwined with the actual steps to wealth, they are not the steps themselves. Those will come in a later section, but the principles described below will help you develop the right attitude which will make following the steps that much easier. Not easy, but easier.

1. **The right concept of Time** – building wealth takes time. Often it takes years. The one who wishes to build wealth should accustom himself to this principle so that his expectations are realistic and therefore valid. The idea that intelligence or excessive effort can outrun time is a false one. Good things take time. Lasting wealth

takes time to build. Think of your wealth-building journey like you would a season in a sports League rather than a championship final. During the season, you will play many matches, you will win some and lose some, there will also be draws. Regardless, you will grow your team, recruit players, sell tickets, grow your franchise, gain new fans. Good things take time, great things take even more time.

2. **Work Ethic** - Don't forget that "from the sweat of thy brow shall thou eat thy bread". A lot of work is required to build anything. Work is the "putting together of things". Everything that has been built was put together. The basic elements are already in existence and they are finite. There is nothing new to be created. Just existing primordial elements to be put together in new forms. There are, for example, only 7 basic musical notes, but the potential combinations are endless.

3. **The Right Attitude to Learning** - learning is lifelong but true knowledge comes from experience, from doing, from repetition and adaptation. The right approach to building wealth is a matter of learning and practice (execution, adaptation and repetition). Although this could (and should) be learnt as early as adolescence, it is however never too late, even if you are just a decade from retirement i.e. if you are already 55 years old, you can start learning to build wealth. 5 – 10 years is ample time to build something substantial. In any case, it would be better than doing nothing. Those who train in the martial arts assert, and as you may have already seen from the movies, that the learning of fighting techniques is usually done by repetition, lots of repetition. However, it is not really a matter of doing thousands of mindless repetitions but about making mindful, conscious attempts at self-observation and self-correction. The key lies in conscious observation, adaptation and absorption of the right principles and

mindset through repetition. Quality not quantity. This is how to learn. It applies to all learning. If you learn to play a musical instrument, your objective is to produce a clear crisp sound from the instrument. When the sound is wrong, you adapt and self-correct (tune the instrument or place your fingers differently etc.), until the right sound or beat is achieved. Learning to build wealth is like this too.

4. **Discipline & Self-control** – it is essential to develop mastery over your desires, mastery over your ego, overcoming your weaknesses (of which laziness and love of ease are probably number one amongst we human beings). Since we agree that building wealth takes sustained activity over time, it should be obvious that discipline is required to follow the programme. Discipline is doing what needs to be done when it needs to be done regardless of emotions or lack of motivation. The sun shines whether it feels like it or not. Most of us only exhibit discipline when it is externally imposed e.g. by your employer or manager at work. Building your own wealth will require you to stick to a plan and execute it regularly, possibly daily, for some time. The good thing though is that when discipline becomes a habit, it becomes easy, really easy and even enjoyable.

5. **Sowing before Reaping** - work and earn before you spend, save, reduce all excess. Do you really need a new smartphone sold to you by someone else lining his own pockets from your confusion, telling you to pay in instalments over a 2-year period? Is your ego so fragile that it needs a shiny new phone to feel happy? Wealth, I assure you, is not built that way. The true cost of buying a new model phone is not the $600 you paid for it, it is not even about the profit you could have made had you invested that money instead. The real cost lies in the depletion of your psyche towards sustainable wealth-building each time you succumb. You will then

need extra mental energy next time to break old habits and develop the right habit. If you have a perfectly functional phone, it is your ego that needs a new one. A fragile ego doesn't build wealth, it consumes it, and very rapidly too!

6. **Cooperation & Clout** – this is the cornerstone stone of wealth; be clear in your mind that you cannot build it alone. Despite there being 8 billion of us living on one tiny planet, our fingerprints and DNA are unique. Does it not make you think? Wherewithal is value. It is the basis of exchange. We must exchange value energy with each other in the form of services or goods. Each human being has a unique energy to contribute to the comity of mankind. This exchange of energy is vital. The energy under your control is your path to wealth, and you don't really own it since you are not on earth forever. You are only a custodian of it and may use it while it is with you. You need others to give you their energy in exchange for yours. The more you give, the more you get in return. What you get in return is your wherewithal, your reservoir of accumulated energy, with which you can procure what you need (goods and services) from others to enhance your life. This principle is a game changer for most people when they imbibe it. It makes wealth-building fun and makes life peaceful and decimates any confusion one may have had about what is required to live joyfully. *But even more noteworthy in this regard is the development of a willingness to give.* Give and give to others. Give wholeheartedly without scheming to receive in return. Just give. It doesn't have to be money. Everyone has something to give, life offers us so many opportunities to give. It may be as simple as offering advice to others or lending a helping hand to mow your elderly neighbour's lawn. Wake up in the morning and consider "what can I offer to my fellow human beings today?" Give and give as much as you can. You will be amazed at how your burdens will be lifted, how

much stronger you will become mentally and how much easier your wealth-building journey will become. You have something unique to give and you have a solemn duty to give it. Don't forget that it was given to you too, a gift from out of the Goodness of Life.

Keep these principles on your mind as you learn the seven wealth-building steps in the next section. Let them sink in and use them to give context to the steps, because if you cannot apply them to your personal circumstances, this will just end up as an academic excursion: interesting but not really of tangible value.

And if it is not tangible, it is not really wealth.

II

SEVEN SIMPLE STEPS TO BUILDING WEALTH

Your Wealth-building Toolkit!

5

STEP 1: DEFINE YOUR VISION OF WEALTH

Strange as it may sound, most human beings have no clear picture of what wealth means for them. Most people are familiar with the stereotypical images of wealth today (super cars, private jets, yachts, luxury penthouse apartments, etc) but these are mostly illusions, and they change with time. For example, a man with excess farm produce was considered rather wealthy at some point in history. In the 1970s, a millionaire was as much a rarity as was private air travel. Nowadays, many of us think you are not wealthy except you are a billionaire! What does your own picture of wealth look like? Take time to reflect on it and document it, let it become a clear picture in your mind's eye. Remember the discussion on the purpose of Wealth in the preceding chapter? Write your future life story with that in mind. What would you like to do every month? Every year? How would you like to live? What kind of diet would you like to follow? What clothes would you like to wear? What kind of house or houses would you like to live in? In which location or locations? Look at the purpose of wealth section in the preceding chapter and design your dream life. Then try to put a cost figure to it in today's terms. Draw the journey to that life from your current life: how old are you now? Are you married or do you hope to be married? Do you have children or hope to have children? How many? If you have children already, how old is the youngest now? When will he/she be 21 years old? If your children are under 5years old or you have none yet, then it makes sense to think of a 4-bed house. If your youngest is already 15, then you will probably be looking to downsize relatively soon, etc. Take a deep look at your life now and connect it to your dream life. Do you wish to be free to travel 5 times a year? Do you want to live in another country? Dream it, but document it and then cost it. How much would you need in yearly income to live this way and still leave a legacy? This is the first step. Wealth cannot be built in a vacuum, neither can life be lived.By simply saving and reducing excess spending, you may already have all you need for a wealthy life within your current income trajectory.

Action Steps:

1. Review the section on the purpose of wealth in chapter 2.
2. Make out time to document your idea of a wealthy life (now is the time to bring together all the entries in your scrapbook, your Pinterest account, etc.)
3. Use the headings in action 1 above as a guide to sort and classify the various aspects of your dream life. An example is shared below using a fictional character Anderson Anoai, a management consultant who lives in Manhattan with his wife and 3 daughters. Andy practises Thai boxing and Yoga (with his wife). He is originally from Tahiti and would like to retire there. Andy needs to earn a little over $70, 000 per annum after tax as a minimum to pursue his dream life. Please feel free to insert or remove anything you want or don't want in your own dream life. The numbers here are not necessarily realistic, this is just to give you a flavour of the

STEP 1: DEFINE YOUR VISION OF WEALTH

process

About you Section (Andy Anoai)	
Age	45
Married or Single	Married
No. of children	3
Age of last child	12 years
Current location	New York
location you'd like to live in	Polynesia
Occupation now	Consultant
dream occupation	Screen Writer

Dream | Future Life Section		
Section	Expense Item	Annual Cost
Shelter	3-bedTownhouse in Manhattan (Mortgage)	$9,800.00
	Villa in Polynesia (dream retirement home) Tahiti	$9,800.00
Nourishment	Couple Yoga retreats (twice a year)	$2,000.00
	Food	$12,000.00
	Medical insurance/ comprehensive Health check-ups, alternative treatments	$12,000.00
Clothing	Regular wardrobe	$6,000.00
	Occasional wardrobe	$6,000.00
Experiencing	Bucket List of 14 countries @ $3500 per year	$3,500.00
	Art collecting	$2,000.00
	Whisky collecting	$500.00
	Entertainment (movie nights, cinema, dinners)	$1,000.00
Legacy	Foundation for preservation of Polynesian Art (investment account)	$2,500.00
	Generational Wealth Investment ($100 per month x 3 children)	$3,600.00
ANNUAL TOTAL		$70,700

6

STEP 2 - GET COMFORTABLE WITH NUMBERS (BUDGETING)

This is the major step to wealth building. If you master this step alone, you will build wealth. Without becoming comfortable with numbers and budgeting, you risk diminishing your current and future financial resources. Ensuring that you have a firm understanding of your income and expenditure is essential to safeguard and potentially enhance your assets in the long run. Most of us have never liked numbers. Math is probably the most disliked school subject on earth. But guess what? It is only numbers that will never lie to you. Numbers are your reality. You don't need to like numbers, but you must get acquainted with and comfortable with them. All you need is basic arithmetic, not algebra or calculus. You only need to be able to subtract, add, multiply and divide. And you don't need to give yourself a panic attack, you can use a calculator. And the greater part of the work you need to do has only to do with documenting stuff. Writing it down. That's all really.

You must know where your money is at all times. This is not as tedious as it sounds at first. I am not proposing that you count your gold coins every night in the candlelight like Silas Marner or log on to your online banking app every hour. It is a simple matter of planning: having a budget and adhering to it. The average human being has wherewithal, he provides something in exchange for income on a regular basis. If what you earn is greater than what you spend, you are already on your way to wealth building.

Most of us have a wrong relationship with money. Virtually everyone believes that money is vital to their survival on earth, yet we refuse to have a practical, healthy relationship with it. We bury our heads in the sand about the things most important to us, our health, our financial situation, etc. Who amongst us is conscious of everything he puts in his mouth? The best of us care about our main meals but we are careless about the snacks we pop into our mouths daily at odd moments. In the same vein, most people are aware of their major expenditures, but not of the various little things we spend on daily, sweets, snacks, drinks, etc. If you don't know where your money goes, you will never control it, it will control you and you will struggle to build true wealth. Not even if you won the lottery. I mean really, really struggle.

It is simple but not easy. It requires a little discipline, that is all. It is in your hands, no matter how little you earn or how huge the debts you have. Even if you have 20 children and 10 ex-wives. Things can be better if you take control of the numbers. At least become aware of the situation, then the opportunities around you will reveal themselves.

Numbers should not also be limited to your current situation; you must use numbers to make sense of your future path as discussed in Step 1.

Ideally your savings should be divided into two pots:

1. Your investment pot (your capital)
2. Your emergency fund (life happens to us all. Expenses come up that are unplanned and necessary. This pot will help you minimize

STEP 2 - GET COMFORTABLE WITH NUMBERS (BUDGETING)

the negative impact.)

Below is a simple budget, again from Andy, that shows how easily you could make a change. Small steps lead to huge changes:

Budget for Anoai Family

Expenditure	Monthly		Annual	
	Planned	Actual	Planned	Actual
Rent/Mortgage	1,500.00	1,500.00	18,000.00	tbc
Property tax	120.00	120.00	1,440.00	tbc
Utilities	350.00	350.00	4,200.00	tbc
Internet	50.00	50.00	600.00	tbc
Mobile Phones *(x 3)*	120.00	120.00	1,440.00	tbc
Car (fuel, taxes)	200.00	200.00	2,400.00	tbc
Car Insurance & Tax	180.00	180.00	2,160.00	tbc
Home Insurance	90.00	90.00	1,080.00	tbc
Additional Medical/Gym	100.00	100.00	1,200.00	tbc
Entertainment/Netflix	75.00	75.00	900.00	tbc
Additional Education *(children)*	120.00	120.00	1,440.00	tbc
Groceries	1,000.00	1,000.00	12,000.00	tbc
Savings *(both Capital and emergency)*	3,000.00	3,000.00	36,000.00	tbc
Total Expenditure		6,905.00	82,860.00	tbc

Income	Monthly		Annual	
	Planned	Actual	Planned	Actual
Salary 1	3,166.00	3,166.00	37,992.00	tbc
Salary 2 *(Malaika's job: school teacher)*	2,350.00	2,350.00	28,200.00	tbc
Muay Thai 3 evenings a week, Malaika teaches yoga on Saturdays)	1,450.00	1,450.00	17,400.00	tbc
Total Income	6,966.00	6,966.00	83,592.00	tbc

Action Steps:

1. Review your income and expenditure and create a budget based on your current situation.
2. Add a savings section and start saving whatever you can afford.
3. Review after one month to see what how you are faring.
4. Repeat Action 3 after 3 months.

7

STEP 3-CREATE A WEALTH-BUILDING LIFESTYLE (SAVING)

To build wealth, you must save, save and save. That is how the building blocks of wherewithal are made. That is why it is called "building wealth". I liken it to building a dam. Picture it yourself; a river is flowing, perhaps trickling, but if you put a dam at some point along the course of the riverflow, the water builds up. The built-up water then rises and can generate greater power, the power of compounding. When the dam is released, it can generate electricity, which it couldn't whilst trickling and flowing away. Getting there takes discipline and patience though, prepare yourself for that. Building anything takes patience, takes time.

Save for what you want. Work and earn before you spend, save, reduce all excess, a spartan life builds character in any case, it builds strength and inner control.

Living a simple life without egotistical vanity is the right way to build wealth. True peace of mind and independence will only come when you liberate yourself from the pressure of vanity. Fretting over how others see you but disguising it as having "refined taste" or "a high sense of beauty" or perhaps as "symbols of accomplishment" will not free you. Perhaps you think driving a fancy car is an accomplishment? You've wanted one for a long time afterall. Now you earn enough to take a loan to buy one. Your friends are impressed, they think you've "arrived", but they only praise your foolishness. The expensive car is most likely a depreciating asset, not an investment. It is also high maintenance. It gives nothing but temporary mental satisfaction. Is that worth sacrificing the chance to save, invest and build lasting wealth and leave a legacy? Is that worth the penury you could possibly experience in your old age, when you can no longer earn a salary?

If you need transportation, there are many less expensive alternatives. Besides, *walking is also good for your health.* Walk more! If you have average health and no locomotive disability, wrap up warm, get comfortable shoes and walk more. Walking has done so much for my physical health. I have also had my greatest inspirations when I walk. Remember that the foundation of your wealth is your physical body. There is no such thing as "arriving in style". Arrive safe and sound, live long and be happy. The idea is safe locomotion. That is all. Everything else is in your imagination alone. Get over it and save yourself grief. Save your money for better things, for the true enjoyment of life. You are not denying yourself luxuries. You are only learning to enjoy the real things; things like the company of people who care about you, nature, a good book, genuine happiness, simple healthy food, love, fresh air, music, clean comfortable accommodation, good health and the liberating feeling of financial security.

Many will say "live a little". True. I am simply asking you to redefine what it is to live. When you do this, foregoing these vanity products will feel more like a cleansing rather than a sacrifice. You will build your wherewithal and simultaneously build peace within. Your relationship with time also changes. You start to recognise that time is going nowhere, and that you were the one running in haste all the while, unnecessary haste too.

STEP 3-CREATE A WEALTH-BUILDING LIFESTYLE (SAVING)

You will eliminate shallow thinking in your life and have a better relationship with money. It is just a tool and nothing more. You will walk tall like a king, even though you have only $10 in your account, you will no longer be afraid of men with earthly power nor will you overly respect people because of money. Your simplicity will set you free.

Action Steps:

1. Read this chapter again. Let it sink in.
2. Make sure you have taken the actions from Step 2 (Budgeting).
3. Carry out a dispassionate review of your current expenditure and identify where you can reduce costs, eliminate the things you don't really need or seek less expensive options to things you think you need. Do your research. You will be amazed at how much is out there.
4. Try your new leaner budget for 3 months and see how you have adjusted and saved more capital.
5. Repeat after 3 months.

8

STEP 4- INVEST (MONEY SHOULD NEVER SLEEP)

Savings alone will not give you enough wherewithal to be truly wealthy and free. In the modern economy, the purchasing power of money reduces over time due to inflation. This is the biggest threat to your savings. The value of your savings must be increasing faster than the rate of inflation, or you would be losing in the long term. The way to do this is to invest your savings, this way your savings, used as capital, will lead to wealth.

Besides, once you stop working and earning, your savings will be rapidly depleted no matter how frugal your lifestyle habits. If you are not earning, your previously earned money must still be earning for you. You cannot leave it to sleep. It will age and deteriorate faster than you will. Your savings would then be like seeds left to rot in a barn. We can also liken the process to sowing and reaping. That is in fact what it is – you must sow, you must continue to water the plant, you must remove weeds that could hinder growth. The seeds will germinate and grow whilst you are asleep or away on holiday, and eventually you will have harvest year-on-year. It is not rocket science, it is very simple. Those who have been truly successful at wealth-building have always

STEP 4- INVEST (MONEY SHOULD NEVER SLEEP)

followed it. Just saving money with a view to saving enough to live on later without working is a flawed strategy because it negates the natural Law of Constant Motion. The Earth never stops spinning, you never stop moving (until you die at least), your money must therefore be working if you are not earning.

Conventional wisdom is that the stock market will always outperform inflation. This is true because the stock market aggregates the constant effort to produce goods and services in an economy, almost all the production in that jurisdiction. The safest way to invest in the stock market is to invest in the major indexes themselves rather than in sectors or particular companies. Companies no matter how old and successful can fail. But the index only fails when the entire country collapses, and that is less likely to occur, besides which if it occurs, you will have other existential matters to deal with rather than your money. Land and real estate have also always consistently been safe investments for long term gain, and they will continue to be so long as there are human beings on earth. All in all, I am not giving you investment advice here, just pointing you in the direction of research. You must do your own research, even if you only research into selecting the right investment adviser. There are so many of them today with access to tremendous amounts of information and analytical tools. AI has taken this research capability to a whole new level too. The main point here is that you must put in some effort into getting your savings to work for you. If you don't want to learn yourself how to do it, at least look into selecting those who can do it for you. You don't need anything fancy, don't go looking for outlandish returns. But seek to build steadily over time. If you have a frugal simple lifestyle, time becomes your friend rather than an enemy.

Action Steps:

1. Do some research into Investing and investment advisers (speak to your bank for starters.)
2. Make sure your savings are going into the most rewarding account type (consider not just the interest rate offered, but any charges for withdrawals and other fees)
3. Decide on an investment plan and start putting the capital part of your savings into the investment plan regularly
4. Set yourself a target date for when you will start investing (say 3 months from today). It doesn't matter how little you invest. Just start. These days you can start with buying as little as one stock in an index or a company you have researched. Then add to your holding every month, whatever you can afford.
5. Review after 3 months

9

STEP 5 - LEAVE NO WEAPON UNDRAWN (USE ALL AVAILABLE RESOURCES)

This step is primarily about demystifying the so-called "side hustle concept", it is about identifying and monetizing what you have within you. The medieval Japanese Swordsman Miyamoto Musashi wrote a treatise (<u>Gorin no Sho, The Book of Five Rings</u>) which is considered one of the greatest books ever written on strategy. In it he advises, amongst other things, that a warrior should not leave the field of battle with part of his arsenal unused. This happens to many of us in life. This is the motivation for this step. We often don't take the time to examine what we have in detail, all the options available to us. We are mostly locked into a tunnel vision of life inculcated in us by society and tradition. We lose battles we could have won if only we drew the various other weapons available to us. To build wealth, you must be all in. First, we must identify what is actually in our arsenal.

Remember in chapter 2 we discussed that wherewithal is value, the basis of exchange. We must exchange energy with each other in the form of service or goods. We also discussed that each human being has a unique energy to contribute to the comity of mankind. Remember there are 8 billion of us, and yet our fingerprints and DNA are unique? There is a unique space and need for your energy- there is a need for you to fulfill, although not necessarily alone, it could be done in concert with others (I would say even best done in concert with others). There is something you have or can do that is unique, either in the way you do it or the level which you can take it to; this lies in the perfection of Creation and of the Creator. Develop that talent into value and exchange it for wherewithal. True entrepreneurship is about discovering the need for that value and fulfilling it. And you don't need to start a separate business for this. There are many vehicles already in existence that you can leverage for this. It could very well be employment or using already established avenues for sharing your knowledge or passion.

Let's say you have been playing Bridge with your friends every weekend for 20 years. That is a lot of experience. You could teach Bridge or embroidery or Chess to others. You could write a book like this one. You can form a social media group for your fellow enthusiasts, and this will only enrich your joy, which is part of your wealth in any case. If you make some more money along the way, then even better. Can you imagine making $100 extra every month for 5 years, doing something that you would have done for free in any case. That seems like a negligible sum at first, but it would amount to $6,000 in those 5 years. With your frugal lifestyle, you would be surviving solely on your salary and could therefore be able to save ALL of that money. If that were invested in the stock market, it could be easily tripled over that time or be ten times greater in value by the time you retire. And all that in addition to whatever else you are able to amass in your wealth dam (pension pot, real estate, etc) and all of this whilst doing something you love. It is so beautiful.

The key principle here is to spend some quality time getting to know yourself so that you can leverage every opportunity available to you; this requires quite deliberate effort. Do not assume that you know yourself, it is very difficult to have an honest opinion of oneself.

How does one do this? Try some or all of the suggestions below.

Action Steps:

1. Ask for honest input from your closest friends and family.
2. List the things that interest you. Those things that just call to your heart. You may not think they have financial value, or you may think those things are commonplace e.g. you love gardening, but so do millions of people. However, remember that each individual is unique. Yes, you too! There is a spin on gardening that is unique to you. You will be surprised that others will find it valuable. You don't even have to plan to monetize it. Just share it with the world. You will be rewarded for it to the level of your genuineness in sharing it. You thereby fulfil the natural Law of Giving and Taking. The more you give the more right you have to take, and the more you will perforce receive and receive in abundance.
3. Spend some time observing how you spend your day over a period, say over a week. Just from when you wake up till when you are in bed. What are the things you like, that you are attracted to. What do you spend your personal time on outside of work? What do you like to watch on TV? What part of a magazine or newspaper do you get drawn to the most – sports, Fashion, interior design, crime, fiction, ecology? Journal all these things for a week and then spend another week ruminating over your notes. Find yourself and know yourself better.

But regardless, you must live a frugal life and not waste your wherewithal. Build it up for when your body will not be as strong, this period (the so-called retirement) is golden. Don't let it become ashen. It is when you will harvest true wisdom from the seeds of the experience sown in your younger years.

10

STEP 6 - STAYING WEALTHY (HOW TO ENJOY AND KEEP IT)

Now you may have gotten the impression from some parts of this book that I advise you to live like a monk who is sour and morose all the time, not really enjoying the luxuries of life. Nothing could be farther from the truth. I do encourage the full and enthusiastic enjoyment of life in all aspects. This is part of the experiencing. However, your enjoyment must not be influenced by uncontrolled vanity and emotions. For enjoyment to be under control, it must be planned for. You must earn the enjoyment first. Enjoyment must not put you in detriment either. It is simple. A fool drinks to excess and then soils his pants and wakes up with a headache that lasts for days. He also damages his health, psyche and reputation. The one who buys a car he can ill afford will suffer consequences that diminish the experience. A friend of mine had a great job. He then developed this desire to buy a Lamborghini. His argument: "you only have one life, enjoy it. There are human beings driving a Lamborghini, why not me?" I have also driven a Lamborghini (rental); they are scintillating to drive. My advice to him was: You don't really need to own one, why not hire one instead, and drive to France (he lives in London) for the weekend with your wife, stay in a luxury hotel, eat gourmet food in a top restaurant, take lots of photos. He only has a good job and a few investments. In a decade he will be unemployable (too old). Enjoy the experience, but don't spend $200,000 to buy a depreciating asset. You get the picture? You can enjoy life, create lovely experiences and still keep your wealth. Unaffordable luxury is self-harm. He went ahead and bought it anyway. When he complains about the haemorrhaging insurance costs and monthly loan repayments, I give him a stern look that says it all!

Let us take another example. This other person is a millionaire. He was interested in private travel but balked (as one should) at the high annual cost of maintaining a private jet. He decided to turn this desire into a business opportunity and started a private jet hire business with $500,000 (leasing the aircraft). Now he and his family can enjoy private travel cost-free from a profitable business (by using the leased aircraft when it is not hired out). This is how wealth is built. This same person wanted to get a prestigious headquarters for his company in Canary Wharf, London. Rather than rent an expensive office, he raised finance to actually purchase a high-rise building (12 floors). His company uses only the 12th floor, where he has his dream penthouse office, but the other 11 floors generate steady rental income meaning he has a profit-generating property and can continue to build lasting wealth, whilst living his dream life. You must think outside the box and not simply follow your emotions.

Action Steps:

1. Review and analyze all your desires (list them out)
2. Cost them and explore other less expensive ways of achieving the same experience.
3. Take the necessary steps to put these into action. Get professional

STEP 6 - STAYING WEALTHY (HOW TO ENJOY AND KEEP IT)

advice if required.

11

STEP 7 - LEGACY: BUILDING GENERATIONAL WEALTH

This expression "generational wealth" has been a buzzword for a few years now, before that we only spoke about "old" and "new" money. The key thing here is legacy. I am not necessarily talking about building a dynasty. However, if you wish to build a dynasty or empire, feel free to do so. You want your wealth to continue to have impact after your departure. The key here lies in helping future generations to understand and master wealth-building from an early age. Remember that wealth-building takes time. The sooner you start the better, the easier and the more wealth you can build. The key is to teach them how; teach them prudence, saving and investment. But you should help them to build it too.

A few points to help you to help them along:

- Put a little away for them from birth or from whenever you can. For example: $50 a month from birth will by age 18 give you about $19, 000 (assuming 5% annual interest, compounded). This is about giving the youngster some capital to start his wealth-building

STEP 7 - LEGACY: BUILDING GENERATIONAL WEALTH

journey with. This is not for splurging on luxury. Remember the frugal approach to wealth- building.
- Encourage your child to continue this trend. If he or she starts putting away an additional $50 (totaling $100 if you maintain your $50) for the next 14 years at the same 5% rate, we are looking $62, 000 by the time this child is 32 years old. Now imagine that you were buying $50 a month of shares in strong reliable companies instead and using a tax-free vehicle (in the UK this would be a Junior ISA but check the options in your own jurisdiction); Guide the child into investing and we could easily be talking about millions by the time he or she is 40.
- The important lessons must be learnt along the way though; healthy frugal living, delayed gratification, a tradition of working hard, saving and investing. If these become your family traditions, you will perpetuate generational wealth in the same way that some families have perpetuated generational poverty (generational blessing versus generational curse.)

Action steps:

1. Do your research and open a savings or investment account for your child as soon as possible.
2. Update your budget to put in a little contribution into it every month.
3. Stick to the plan and review after a couple of years.
4. Start teaching your child about saving and delayed gratification today. Let him or her understand how to maintain a balanced outlook and resist peer pressure.
5. As part of your future dream life exercise in Step 1, you should have put some thought into your legacy. Now is the time to flesh

out the plans for this and start working towards it. You may wish to open a separate investment account for this. Contribute to it regularly and continue to refine it.

6. Estate Planning: it also makes sense to plan for when you are no longer around to take care of your family. Consider a life insurance policy and smart structure for your assets that make inheritance easier. The key thing here is to ensure your affairs are in order and your dependants (as well as your legacy) are protected from foreseeable losses in the event of your sudden departure. Consider getting professional advice on how to do these things or carry out your own research to understand the intricacies of the jurisdiction you live in. This is part of protecting your legacy too.

12

CONCLUSION: A FINAL WORD

Now you know what to do. This book has been deliberately kept rather short and concise. Nevertheless, there is a lot of work to do, a lot of research into specifics, but most importantly actions to take. Like I mentioned in the Foreword, I have only highlighted principles that are simple and commonsensical. I have probably told you nothing so new as to be startling, since these are very natural and accessible principles. Wealth-building does not require genius, just discipline and consistency, staying power and a focused attitude. You will likely feel motivated to take action now. I encourage you to do so, but don't rush, learn to walk before trying to run. Motivation and inspiration alone will not build wealth, you need a huge dose of discipline to achieve consistency. Besides, motivation doesn't last forever I'm afraid, you need discipline for when the rose-tinted glasses crack. Believe me, they will. Follow the simple rules and stick to them. Keep your eye on the numbers, stick to your budget and buy all means set targets for yourself. They are milestones on the way that will validate the actions you are taking, assuring you of steady progress.

However, I must point out that a watched pot never boils. Do not fret about wealth-building. I have advised keeping an eye on the numbers, but you must give it time too. For investments, the frequency of your review at most should be quarterly. And don't worry that the value is increasing so slowly, as long as it is on the upward trajectory, you are on the right path.

Reward yourself every now and then too. But make sure you budget for it. Plan for it. Don't make yourself miserable trying to build wealth. By all means, live well and enjoy the simple things of life. Live life, learn from life and love life.

Life and love are really all the wealth we need.

I promised a recap of the principles in this book. Here goes:

	The Purpose of Wealth		Principles to note
1	Shelter	1	Time - lasting wealth takes time to build
2	Nourishment	2	Work ethic
3	Clothing	3	Learning Attitude
4	Experience	4	Discipline and Self-control
5	Legacy	5	Save, earn before you buy
		6	Cooperation & Clout building
The Seven Steps To Wealth-Building			
Step 1	Define Your Vision of Wealth		
Step 2	Get Comfortable with Numbers (Budgeting)		
Step 3	Create A Wealth-Building Lifestyle (Saving)		
Step 4	Invest (Money Should Never Sleep)		
Step 5	Leave No Weapon Undrawn (Use All Available Resources)		
Step 6	Staying Wealthy (How to Enjoy and Keep It)		
Step 7	Legacy: Building Generational Wealth		

I hope you found this book helpful. I'd be grateful if you could take a few minutes to leave an honest review on Amazon.

Good luck!

13

Suggested Reading

In Chapter 2, I alluded to a book that has helped me to shape my view of life. I must point out from the outset that it is not about wealth-building, but rather a book that describes life and existence in its entirety. In my opinion, it answers the many questions that engage the mind of any deep-thinking person.

I heartily recommend the book:

"In the Light of Truth", The Grail Message written by Abd-ru-shin and published by Alexander Bernhardt Publishing Company, Vomperberg, Austria.

Website: www.alexander-bernhardt.com

DISCLAIMER

Although I have already mentioned it several times in this book, it is important to state here formally that no part of this book should be construed as offering financial or investment advice. The principles shared in this book are for educational purposes only. Please seek professional financial advice for any investments you choose to make.

About the Author

AMD has over 30 years of management experience mostly in the Financial services sector, during which career he has worked on some of the biggest M&A integration projects in European banking history.

Since childhood, he has had an innate desire to understand the "Nature of Things". This desire manifests in what many consider to be an uncanny ability to see patterns in life. In this book, having been urged by close friends to do so, he shares simple principles about wealth-building, thus making them accessible to anyone with a genuine interest in the topic.

www.ingramcontent.com/pod-product-compliance
Lightning Source LLC
Chambersburg PA
CBHW030512220526
45464CB00006B/2769